Jim Forgetting

# Jim Forgetting

Col Cseke

*Jim Forgetting*
first published 2013 by
Scirocco Drama
An imprint of J. Gordon Shillingford Publishing Inc.
© 2013 Col Cseke

Scirocco Drama Editor: Glenda MacFarlane
Cover design by Terry Gallagher/Doowah Design Inc.
Author photo by Anton deGroot
Printed and bound in Canada on 100% post-consumer recycled paper.

We acknowledge the financial support of the Manitoba Arts Council and The Canada Council for the Arts for our publishing program.

All rights reserved. No part of this book may be reproduced, for any reason, by any means, without the permission of the publisher. This play is fully protected under the copyright laws of Canada and all other countries of the Copyright Union and is subject to royalty. Changes to the text are expressly forbidden without written consent of the author. Rights to produce, film, record in whole or in part, in any medium or in any language, by any group amateur or professional, are retained by the author.
Production inquiries should be addressed to:
col.cseke@yahoo.ca

Library and Archives Canada Cataloguing in Publication

Cseke, Col, 1984-
    Jim forgetting / Col Cseke.

 A play.
ISBN 978-1-897289-91-4

    I. Title.

PS8605.S43J54 2013      C812'.6      C2013-901302-4

J. Gordon Shillingford Publishing
P.O. Box 86, RPO Corydon Avenue, Winnipeg, MB Canada R3M 3S3

*Jim Forgetting* is dedicated to my Mom and my Nana, who taught me what love, commitment, and care really mean.

# Acknowledgements

My deepest gratitude is owed to the Young Onset Dementia Support Group based in Calgary, AB whose lives greatly informed *Jim Forgetting*. Thanks as well to Jamie Dunsdon, Haysam Kadri, Shawna Burnett, Gordon Pengilly and the Alberta Playwrights Network Playwrighting Circle, Dr David Hogan, Dr Teri Green, and Tessa Kleissen.

## Production History

*Jim Forgetting* premiered March 21, 2012, produced by Verb Theatre in Calgary, Alberta, with the following cast:

JIM .................................................................................. Haysam Kadri

DONNA ........................................................................Shawna Burnett

Directed by Jamie Dunsdon

Note about punctuation:
- / indicates overlapping dialogue
- \- indicates one character interrupting the other

## Col Cseke

Col Cseke is a playwright and performer. He is the Co-Artistic Director of Verb Theatre, where *Jim Forgetting* premiered in 2012. Col has premiered new work, as either a playwright or collective member, at One Yellow Rabbit's High Performance Rodeo, Alberta Theatre Projects playRites Festival, The Calgary International Children's Festival, among others. His plays include *The Dandelion Project* and the book and lyrics for *The Ex-Pats*. As a member of the award winning Downstage Creation Ensemble, Col has co-created and performed in *In The Wake, Good Fences, Bus(t)*, and *Arm's Length Embrace*. Along with his friends at Downstage Col shares three Betty Mitchell Award nominations for Best New Play, with one win for *In The Wake*. Col often creates work with various community groups, collaborating with mixed-ability ensembles, folks who've experienced homelessness, and kids. Col lives in Calgary with his wife Ellen with whom he co-produces The Magpie Treasure Talks speaking series.

# Prologue

*JIM and DONNA are playing crib. JIM is counting points.*

JIM: Fifteen two, fifteen four, fifteen six, and the run is nine. I win.

DONNA: You win.

JIM: OK.

DONNA: OK, we should get going.

JIM: We're just getting going. We should play another game.

*DONNA gives in, JIM begins to shuffle the cards. DONNA moves and speaks to the audience.*

DONNA: I hadn't played cards much before I married Jim. I had never gambled.

*JIM, as he shuffles, reads sentences written on the cards.*

JIM: "Oh I get it, you're joking. I'm like a joke."

DONNA: Since Jim's been sick, though, I've reached for that crib board every time things look like they're slipping away. Like today.

I don't understand it. With everything going on in his mind he never missed a point. He'll forget my name, his name, everything important, but not how to play cards.

*Jim Forgetting*

JIM: "*How can they ask me to talk about my problems. All my problems are sitting next to me, she can hear.*" When I was first, um…

DONNA: Sick?

JIM: Sick. Sick?

DONNA: After Jim was diagnosed he carried with him these cards.

JIM: "*His world has become so small, and he looks small too.*"

DONNA: You'd play games with yourself. Right, remember? Jim? Jim?

JIM: Yeah.

DONNA: Memory games, right? He'd see how many cards in sequence he could remember. Like an exercise. A ten card day would be a, a—

JIM: "*I feel like I've betrayed him. Like I failed.*"

DONNA: Those were wonderful days. And a two card day felt unlucky. But what he's reading now, they're um… When we went to that support group, do you remember Jim?

JIM: How many do you want?

DONNA: We would sit in the circles and the other people there would say things. Things known but, unimaginable.

JIM: Don't interrupt. "*I hate my voice now, it's grown so tiny.*"

DONNA: They'd say things Jim wanted to keep.

JIM: Yeah things I want to keep.

DONNA: Jim?

JIM: But I didn't have a notebook to keep them in.

DONNA: But...

JIM: But I had my pocket cards. When I heard something from the circle I wanted to keep I would write it down on a card. These cards. I had a new memory game. I wasn't remem, mem member, membering, umm, ka, ka k,ki,k—

DONNA: Cards or sequences—

JIM: Kings or Queens or eights or fives or tens or...

DONNA: He was remembering their stories. Or trying to. But he was always at least reading their sentences.

JIM: Play a game with me.

DONNA: At first I treasured these crib matches, to see him be himself. But I don't think that's really Jim, it's just a reflex. It's like these games are just bumping him in the knee with a little mallet.

*DONNA starts turning over cards.*

A club to be battered with.

A spade to be gutted by.

A flattened heart.

A fake and hollow diamond.

Everywhere I look I see a subtle, violent betrayal. And his handwritting on them is frantic and ugly.

JIM: Let's play.

DONNA: We've been playing this game for hours. I'm thinking of the last twelve months and I realize that even my memory of it is incomplete. Jim's disease has eroded big paths of our marriage and left us with just the sharp edges. They're disconnected and painful to touch on, and I can't make sense of what's happened. Oh shit, I'm taking too much time. If I'm, if this is going to happen it has to happen now.

JIM: One more game?

DONNA: Jim we don't have any more time.

JIM: I'll let you win.

DONNA: Really?

JIM: No.

DONNA: OK. We can play again.

JIM: Who deals?

DONNA: Winner deals.


# MARCH

*DONNA is reading. JIM is practicing memorizing cards in sequence.*

JIM: Ten of spades, six of spades...eight of...hearts? And... Shit.

*JIM reshuffles the cards, reads ten or so, and tries again.*

Clubs Queen diamonds five hearts ace hearts six clubs, clubs, clubs...clubs.

*JIM gives up.*

Is that book fun?

DONNA: What? No sweetie it's just—it's boring.

JIM: What is it?

DONNA: Just about the brain.

JIM: Really?

DONNA: Yeah like, how it works and, you know, stuff like that.

JIM: I can read it when you're done?

DONNA: If you want.

JIM: Are you almost done?

DONNA: Not really. Sorry.

JIM: OK. You could read it.

DONNA: I am sweetie.

JIM: Out loud I mean, so we can both read it.

DONNA: It's not like a story.

JIM: No I know Donna, I'm not five years old yet, I don't need to be read a story. But I…

DONNA: *(Not listening.)* What?

JIM: I feel like I used to know this.

DONNA: What?

JIM: How a brain works, the medical, medically I…

DONNA: Oh you do. You're a paramedic. I'm reading this just so I can know some of the things you know.

JIM: OK.

DONNA: But you're right, I can read it out loud, to refresh your memory. OK?

JIM: OK.

DONNA: OK. "Case study number five. Alzheimer's and dementia attack indiscriminately; the ex-Premier known as King Ralph is already displaying signs of his mounting dementia, his once sharp tongue now severly dulled. Soon the disease will take most of his speech, his personality, and his persona. His world is shrinking, and sadly, he shrinks too." [1]

JIM: Can you start from the beginning? Please.

DONNA: Sure. "Introduction: What to Gain From Memory Loss. Many of us are unable to accurately picture a human brain in our mind's eye. Often we think of the brain as small and one dimensional, an illustration in a book. But to understand Alzheimer's is to understand the brain, imagine it—"

Am I reading too fast?

JIM: Keep going.

DONNA: Sorry. "To understand Alzheimer's is to understand the brain. Imagine it this way; the human brain is roughly the size an adult man makes when holding his two fists together.

> *JIM holds his fists together. He stops listening to DONNA's reading. He is engrossed in his fists and then begins to make hand puppets, calling out their names, dancing around the room.*

"A healthy brain would appear meaty and firm. An Alzheimer's-riddled brain, by comparison, is covered with plaques and tangles, restricting blood flow and disrupting neuron connections."

JIM: Rabbit. Look, a rabbit.

DONNA: "Keep in mind that although these plaques and tangles are the physical causation of Alzheimer's disease, the disease is not a thing; it is a process. The term Alzheimer's disease itself is merely a diagnostic emblem."

---

1   See Appendix B for optional text.

JIM:     Huh? A crocodile.

DONNA:   Huh? Um, "You know now, more than anyone, how this process of Alzheimer's is beginning to affect your loved one. It's tempting to focus on what Alzheimer's takes from a person; their capabilities, their personality, their sense of self."

JIM:     Horse. Huh? A horse. Kind of, I guess.

DONNA:   It's good. "But what you'll need to do to survive this ordeal is to focus on what you can prevent the disease from taking from your loved ones and what it gives to them. Some see Alzheimer's as giving a unique type of creativity to sufferers. It does not have to take their joy in life. It does not have to take the love you feel for each other. It does not have to take their..."

> *JIM is fighting to find the name of his last hand puppet.*

JIM:     B...B-b-b-b-

DONNA:   That's a bird Jim.

JIM:     B-b-b-b—

DONNA:   Bird. Jim bird.

JIM:     B... B...

DONNA:   Bird.

JIM:     Butterfly!

> *JIM is triumphant.*

## SEPTEMBER

*Middle of the night. JIM runs into the room, panicked, rubbing his eyes.*

JIM: What the, oh god. Fuck…

*DONNA enters after him*

DONNA: Jim? What's the matter?

JIM: Look here Donna, look at my face, / is it OK?

DONNA: / You bolted out of bed like you were on fire.

JIM: Fire?

DONNA: No, no fire, calm down.

JIM: These fucking nightmares Donna.

DONNA: Oh sweetie. It's OK now. They're getting that bad? What happened?

JIM: I can't tell, I don't know. They're not…they're so strong they wake me up, but as soon as I'm up I can't remember half of them. But I do remember these fucking intense, weird tiny portions of them, but with no context. But they're vivid. I thought my eyelashes were on fire, that's what woke me up.

DONNA: That's horrifying.

JIM: I opened my eyes and I thought I saw little flames coming off of my face and it was like I could smell my eyelashes burn. It was so real, but, but I don't know what happened before that, in the dream, I don't know what set me on fire. I'm losing my mind. Something must have happened. Something wild and scary and real must have happened in my dream and I have no clue. How could I imagine something that terrible and only remember the end.

DONNA: You probably don't want to remember it.

JIM: I just want to sleep, even if it means dreaming this shit. I spend most of the night lying there trying to think of what woke me.

DONNA: You usually fall asleep before I do.

JIM: I'm exhausted so I'm out at first but, but I'm up four or five times every night. During the day too, I catch myself thinking about it, or trying to, or drifting off, or. I just want to fucking sleep.

DONNA: Me too, Love. Here, come back to bed.

JIM: I think I'll stay up for a while, I don't want to just lie in bed getting pissed off I'm not sleeping. I do love, though, hearing you sleep.

DONNA: Oh.

JIM: I get a bit jealous, but your breath is so peaceful. It's comforting.

DONNA: Then come lie down with me, and in the morning we'll get you an appointment with Dr. Faisal. We need to push her—

JIM: There's no sense in it, we've done enough tests. If they haven't figured out what's wrong yet it has to mean that there's nothing medical going on. It's just— I don't know, it's just in my head. It's just thinking about not sleeping makes me not sleep, and thinking about stress makes me stressed.

DONNA: But it's more than just the sleeping. Come lie down, try and clear your mind, and we'll talk about it in the morning.

JIM: Clear my mind? Like it's that easy.

## DECEMBER

> *JIM enters with a brochure and a sheet of paper with handwritten notes on it. He refers to the sheet throughout the scene.*

JIM: Donna? Here.

DONNA: What's this?

JIM: Look at this. It's a brochure for the extended care unit at Memorial.

DONNA: 'Kay.

JIM: That's where I'd like to go.

DONNA: What?

JIM: So I went and looked at all of the places I could maybe go and this is what I think would be my favorite./ It's nice. My insurance would cover most of it and it just got renovated, it's not as old looking as a lot of the places I saw. And I, would you stop? Stop. Stop talking!

DONNA: /Jim. Jim this is so beyond… Jim we don't need to be thinking about this right now. What are you talking about? What?

JIM: *(Looking at his sheet.)* I just need to get through this please. I can't, I'll lose track if you're talking over me like that. Don't.

DONNA: Sorry.

JIM: Just listen please.

DONNA: I don't understand why you're thinking about this right now. We don't need it.

JIM: I want to be the one to pick where I'll end up. And I need to do it while I can still make good decisions. I, I don't mind this place. Read the brochure, I like it. It's nice. And I was thinking that maybe they'll let me help out if I can, maybe part of me will still remember some of my paramedic training.

*Looking at his sheet.*

I read that sometimes things that were learnt before the Alzheimer's starts to show can, can be retained. I read about this woman who has it pretty bad but she still remembers Latin from when she was a World War Two nurse. Maybe I can kind of work there when I move in there.

DONNA: OK. I totally get that. Let's volunteer there.

JIM: That's not it.

DONNA: We both can, we should, I think that's great. I'll go with you.

JIM: No. You can't...come. You shouldn't go there at all.

DONNA: What?

JIM: I don't think you should ever walk in there.

DONNA: So you think I can just, what, drop you off at the door, just slow down the car and roll you out so I can forget about you? Fine. I won't go there because you're not going there. You're not going anywhere Jim. This is our home. / You're just scared Jim, that's fine. If you want to volunteer then we can, I think that's great, but you're not living in a hospital. You're not going there Jim! I'm sure it's nice but the people there are just there until they die and you don't get to pick that! You don't get to just paint your tongue black and wait to die. You don't bring home a brochure. Thinking like that's just, it's not helping anything. It's defeatist. You may as well write your own fucking obituary then. You're scared. You're just scared.

JIM: /Not for too much longer. We both know I can only last just so long here, you'll only last so long, there's no use in denying it. This is where I should…I said don't talk over me Donna! Don't—

But am I wrong?

DONNA: I won't do it Jim. I'm not dumping you there. I need you here.

JIM: *(Looking at the sheet.)* I'm not saying I need to go there tomorrow but there is going to come a point where—

DONNA: What's that paper?

JIM: Just some notes. I didn't want to forget anything I wanted to say. I'm not saying that I need to go there tomorrow, but there is going to come a point Donna where you'll stop being my wife, all you'll be to me is a nurse. I won't remember to even say thank you.

DONNA: You'll always be my husband, you'll always be the person I'm married to.

JIM: But I won't love you anymore. To me you'll just be a nurse who I hardly recognize. When that happens send me here, let nurses be nurses.

*Gives her the brochure. Looks at his sheet.*

Once I go don't come see me. If you can stop yourself from coming to see me you can forget me. If you stop yourself from visiting me, all you'll have is a memory of me. And that'll go. That's nothing.

DONNA: I'm not going to do it Jim.

JIM: I know I can be difficult. No one will blame you for it. Everyone would know it's the only thing to do.

DONNA: I don't care about that, I don't—

| | |
|---|---|
| JIM: | And don't worry about being alone. |
| DONNA: | What? |
| JIM: | You won't be alone. |
| DONNA: | What? |
| JIM: | *(Looking at his sheet.)* You should go back to Dan. I checked, he's single. |
| DONNA: | Don't. |
| JIM: | I know he'd want to be with you. I never said it but he's a good… He's… It's pretty obvious that if you hadn't been with me you'd have been with him. Well, you're not really going to be with me much longer, so…go. |
| DONNA: | Why are you saying this? |
| JIM: | It's not easy, but… |
| DONNA: | Jim? |
| JIM: | You shouldn't be alone just 'cause of this and me and… |
| DONNA: | When I…when what happened with Danny and me happened you didn't leave me. You should have, I didn't deserve you. How could I leave you now Jim? |
| JIM: | But I still had you. I, umm, I don't think you get to keep me much longer. |

*JIM is studying his sheet.*

| | |
|---|---|
| DONNA: | What do your notes say? |
| JIM: | It just says "too humiliating." |
| DONNA: | Oh. |
| JIM: | I don't know if I meant you or me. |

## MAY

> DONNA is rummaging through a box full of mementos from her wedding with JIM. She pulls out a number of keepsakes, and then finds two discs, a CD and a DVD. She puts on the CD and as Louis Armstrong's "A Kiss to Build a Dream On" plays, she dances for a few seconds to it. She then takes the DVD and goes to another room, leaving the song playing.
>
> JIM enters, he hears the song and hums along with the tune.

**JIM:** Ahh I love this song. But not the song, the...what? The song that this song was, no this song was... Donna? Hey, Donna who is this song?

> DONNA slides the DVD into the player and it begins to load.

Um, I know this song. I should remember this song to get Donna to tell me what it is.

"And my imagination, to bah badum badum" fuck umm. Ahh. Ahah.

> While singing along he pulls out his marker and goes to write on one of his cards, but the marker is dry. JIM rummages through a door and pulls out a digital camera. While this is happening the DVD player plays a home movie from JIM and DONNA's ten-year anniversary party.

On screen:

"Hey, would you turn the music down? Thanks. Hi everyone, thank-you all so much for coming today, I just want to say something quick. Donna. I love you so much, Donna. I know that I love you more than I ever thought I could, but today, on our tenth anniversary, with all of our friends and family and loved ones, and these little *guys running around, hi Peyton. Hi. Say hi to Uncle Jim? With everyone here, especially seeing my parents, who just had you, what Dad? How many years."*

Dad: 38 years.

*"Just had their 38th anniversary, round of applause folks!"*

Cheers.

*"With everyone here, I realize that I thought I couldn't love you any more, but actually, I love you less."*

Chuckles.

DONNA: You little shit./

DONNA: /"Pardon me?"

*In the other room JIM has a digital camera.*

JIM: I'll remember this song.

*JIM takes a photo of the CD player.*

There. Donna will know. Donna, do you remember this song? I think, sometime somewhere maybe we danced to this song.

*Looking at the camera.*

How do you zoom?

*Back in the other room, DONNA is watching the video. Over the course of JIM's speech she begins to quietly sob.*

*I love you less. I love you less today than I will tomorrow. And I love you much less than I will when we're celebrating our 38th. I love you less because I will love you more and more, everyday. C'mon dear, come up here.*

*DONNA comes on screen, they kiss.*

*Jim Forgetting*

JIM: Hey Dad, put on our song.

> They begin to dance to "A Kiss to Build a Dream On."
>
> DONNA, now heavily crying, leaves the room. JIM enters just after her, carrying the camera. He sees the video playing.

Whoa, Donna. Look at you my love. Wait, who, who are you dancing with? Is it?

> JIM takes a photo of himself, and checks the camera.

Oh good, it's me. But, wait, that's not my smile.

> JIM takes another photo of himself, smiling widely.

That's not how I smile.

> JIM takes another photo of himself, with a pained, grotesque smile.

That's not my fucking smile! No, don't zoom.

> JIM feels his mouth tenderly. He looks back at the video playing of them dancing.

Who are you dancing with?


# APRIL

> JIM is eating chocolate, giggling at DONNA, who is looking for her car keys.

DONNA: Have you seen my keys? Jim, could you help look?

JIM: No, of course not.

DONNA: Where are...we should call my parents and tell

|          | them we're going to be late. Hope we don't miss the Easter egg hunt. |
|---|---|
| JIM: | No no. |
| DONNA: | Peyton and Brett will be there, remember them? Peyton is five, and Brett's three. Do you remember them? |
| JIM: | Yes. |
| DONNA: | Jim, try to think, where could my keys have gone? Think about it right now, if you were going to put a set of keys somewhere right now, where would you put them? |
| JIM: | I can't tell you. |
| DONNA: | No huh? |
| JIM: | No. |

*DONNA finds one key on a key ring.*

| DONNA: | Jim? Why is the mailbox key under here? |
|---|---|
| JIM: | Good work. |
| DONNA: | Did you put this here? Hey, look at me. I must have had a dozen keys on my key ring, where are they all? |
| JIM: | You have to find, you're not even looking. Try. |
| DONNA: | Why would you— |
| JIM: | Chocolate? |
| DONNA: | I don't like chocolate. |
| JIM: | You probably couldn't find them anyway. You're slow, I'm too good. We should go. |
| DONNA: | I know, but unless you tell me where my keys are we're stuck. |

| | |
|---|---|
| JIM: | We should go now. I shouldn't be late, if I'm late it'll be terrible. I have to hide my chocolates for Peyton and Brett. |
| DONNA: | What? Oh, do you think…are you, an Easter Bunny? |
| JIM: | Shhh. You can't tell anyone. |
| DONNA: | I don't want to tell anyone. |
| JIM: | I'm the best. It takes years to find my eggs. After I hide it even I can't find them. |
| DONNA: | Shit. |
| JIM: | Don't tell anyone, it's a secret. If you tell them it ruins the surprise. 'Cause when they find them on their own the kids are so happy and they eat it and they get these chocolate bruises, um bruises, or um— |
| DONNA: | Smudges. |
| JIM: | Smudges, on their chins. So we should go. |
| DONNA: | I don't, I don't think we'll go Jim. It's just not a good day for it. I'll umm, I'll call Mom and she can hide the eggs for you, OK, she can substitute for you. |
| JIM: | Oh, alright. |
| DONNA: | I'm sorry. |
| JIM: | If she hides them could you tell her to keep them pretty low? |
| DONNA: | Sure. |
| JIM: | If she hides them too high they won't be found, surprises are no fun if kids can't reach them, then they're just secrets. |
| DONNA: | Hey, you OK? You may not remember but we |

| | |
|---|---|
| | actually have a rule about not having any secrets. Not that you ever did, aside from this whole Easter bunny thing. But I had some secrets Jim that really hurt us and you and, so we made a rule, we banned secrets. |
| JIM: | I don't hide things to be tricky, I just like surprises. |
| DONNA: | You're becoming such a mystery to me Jim. It's exciting, in its way. Like a hunt. Is that what I am to you? Jim? Something to hunt? A prize you see in the distance and you get to spend all day tracking it down. I just wish I was as fascinating to you as you are to me. |
| JIM: | Chocolate? |

## JULY

*JIM is trimming a Christmas tree, Christmas carols are playing. DONNA enters.*

| | |
|---|---|
| DONNA: | `What are you...? Where'd you get all this? |
| JIM: | I brought it up from the basement, thought I'd get an early start on decorating. |
| DONNA: | You sure did. Jim, it's not even six, how long have you been up? |
| JIM: | I'm not sure. Sorry I didn't wait for you. |
| DONNA: | I'm not mad, just surprised. |
| JIM: | I know you don't love the artificial tree. I was thinking about getting a real one this year, but I don't know, plastic ones can be tradition too. |
| DONNA: | It's OK, the real ones just die anyways. Can I help? |

JIM: You can finish the ornaments.

DONNA: Great.

JIM: We need to go pick up some more tinsel though, I'll run out quick and grab some.

DONNA: Later dear, it's umm, it's freezing out and nothing's open yet.

JIM: Yeah good call. Do we have any hot chocolate?

DONNA: Oh, I don't think so.

JIM: OK.

*DONNA pulls out a particular ornament.*

Hey hold on, here, I always hang that one next to this one.

DONNA: How come?

JIM: Well. Nana used to give me an ornament for Christmas every year, but when I was in grade five Nana thought I deserved two.

DONNA: Why?

JIM: I used to have, uh, this is a bit gruesome, sorry, but I had a gerbil when I was a kid. One day, we're not sure how, but it got his leg caught in its wheel and was stuck, so it gnawed its leg off.

DONNA: Jim, that's gross.

JIM: Yeah my Dad was going to kill it, put it out of it's misery, but I thought I could fix it. It didn't bleed a lot and it was pretty calm, so I wrapped his hip with a rubber band and I wrapped up the stump with Kleenex. And I would crush up Tylenol and mixed it with water and I'd rub it onto it's gums with a Q-tip.

DONNA: That's sweet.

JIM: It died in a couple of weeks. Nana said though that even though I couldn't save it that I did a good thing and that she was proud.

DONNA: This is unbelievable.

JIM: Call my Mom if you don't believe me.

DONNA: No I—

JIM: Hey, I talked to Mom this morning, she wants us to do Christmas Eve and Christmas morning at their place again. Is that alright? She likes us there for breakfast. Then do your family for dinner?

DONNA: Sounds great. Your Mom's breakfasts were, are, amazing. Why don't I make us a breakfast like hers this morning?

JIM: Yeah. Hey, you know what, why don't we, let's go get a tree right now. A real one. We'll go cut down a huge bright tree. Do we own an axe?

DONNA: Jim we've never cut down a tree in our lives, I don't think this is the year to start.

JIM: No I did once. In grade six, I had friends who were twins and their Dad took me and them out to some mountain once and we picked a tree out of a forest.

DONNA: Is that real?

JIM: Yeah. It had snowed the night before but when we went it was really sunny. Their Dad would do this awesome thing where he'd make it snow. He'd have us stand under a tree and then he'd shake the hell out of the trunk and all the snow on the boughs would shake off and it would pile down on us. And the sun was so bright all of the snow would just shine. Kevin and I spent most of the day running at trees and dropkicking them so that we'd fall on our backs and catch the snow on our tongues. And we'd stub our toes and we'd be happy.

DONNA: What else did you guys do?

JIM: Me and Kevin used to do lots of stupid shit back then. We did this thing where we'd take off our ski gloves and go like this with our hand to a pine tree.

> *JIM slaps the back of one of his hands into the other palm.*

And we'd get like dozens of tiny tiny little pricks in the back of our hands, but you couldn't really see them at first, then we'd windmill our arms around and all the blood would rush into our hands and then our hands would be covered in all these tiny blood spots. Like mini bullet holes riddling our hands. It looked really, umm…and we would just look at them. And then we'd lick the back of our hands, do girls do that? Boys love the taste of blood, that irony taste and it would kind of taste like pine too from the needles.

> *JIM slaps the back of his hand a few times against the fake tree and then windmills his arm around. It's uncomfortable. He looks at his bloodless hand.*

Not the same when it's fake.

I don't really know why boys do shit like that. I guess it didn't really hurt, which is probably why we did it. A kid thinks that bleeding should hurt, that getting hurt or injured means blood right? But this wasn't really an injury, it was just a kind of slow ache.

But umm, no. It umm. You know it was just one of those things that you know you probably shouldn't do but you can't see any immediate harm in it, so you do.

Umm.

Hey, what do you want for Christmas.

DONNA: Oh, nothing.

JIM: Come on, you always say that.

DONNA: I want…I want a real tree.


# JUNE

*DONNA is sitting in the kitchen. JIM enters.*

JIM: Morning dear. Coffee?

DONNA: Are you asking if there is any or if I want any?

JIM: Uh, I just, what?

DONNA: We finished the pot, you can make a fresh one.

JIM: What's wrong, why are you mad?

DONNA: Nothing.

JIM: Oh shit.

DONNA: Nothing.

JIM: I know what that means.

DONNA: Do you?

JIM: I think so.

DONNA: Look, we had a fight last night, OK? It's fine, I'm fine, just give me a rest for a bit this morning OK?

JIM: We, like, us?

DONNA: Yes Jim, us. We fight.

JIM: I know. Umm…sorry.

DONNA: Sorry? What are you sorry for?

JIM: I don't know.

DONNA: Then don't say sorry. Just don't say anything.

JIM: Do we fight a lot though?

DONNA: Yeah. No, not a lot, but…yeah.

JIM: Well OK then I'm sorry if I don't remember fighting with you last night. I'm sure I did something wrong and I was wrong, and, so yeah.

DONNA: I don't want to keep fighting, and I don't want to keep fighting about fights you don't even remember.

JIM: Well then good, but if you don't want to talk about it then don't get mad.

DONNA: I'm not mad.

JIM: You look mad.

DONNA: I'm allowed to get mad Jim.

JIM: See.

DONNA: Jim.

JIM: And I'm allowed to forget.

DONNA: I know alright, but that doesn't mean it doesn't hurt. I can still be hurt by you.

JIM: How can I hurt you, if I don't even know—

DONNA: We're married.

JIM: You're the one in control here, so just don't let it get to you.

DONNA: I don't have control here.

JIM: More than I do. I'm just saying help me out a bit.

DONNA: That's all I do. And I know, you're allowed to be helpless, so fucking helpless, but still—

JIM: I don't remember what we fought about last night, but I remember fighting with you before and I know you can get mean.

DONNA: I wasn't mean last night I was just upset.

JIM: I remember you saying that before too.

DONNA: I'm sorry Jim, I'm not perfect at this. I still get to be the small one sometimes.

JIM: I don't think you're perfect.

DONNA: But that's what you're demanding.

JIM: How am I demanding anything—

DONNA: I don't mean you. I mean the situation is demanding it. See that's what I'm talking about, I have to say everything exactly as I mean it, there's no room for any sort of vagueness anymore. It's like you just learnt English. Do you know I feel like my vocabulary has shrunk these past months, that I've been dumbed down by this? And for what? We fought last night and you forgot, we're fighting now and you'll forget. You get off scot free and I feel like shit all day.

JIM: I don't get off free! It's a fucking minefield every time I see you in a bad mood because I don't know why you're mad at me but I know something happened. You have a beautiful smile Donna/

DONNA: /Don't try and flatter—

JIM: But you can't fake it worth shit. I know when you're

|   |   |
|---|---|
|   | mad alright. I might not remember things but I can still read a room. And fine, I understand that you're allowed to be mad. But if you are you have to tell me about it. |
| DONNA: | How can I tell you about it without hurting you? Do you know how many times a week you tell me you want to kill yourself? Or that you want us to go visit your dead parents for lunch? Or how often you remember an affair from five years ago and that you hate me? And it hurts me every time, and it makes me mad. You want me to tell you about that? |
| JIM: | No. |
| DONNA: | I don't want to be mad, but I am. Oh God. Everytime I feel something authentic I feel instantly terrible about it. What do I do? I know I shouldn't unload on you like this. I wish that I could tell you about everything that happens around here, I don't have anyone else to talk to, no one I know understands. Not that you understand. |
| JIM: | No, it's um, it's OK to say these things out loud. Umm, what are we fighting about, what did I do? |
| DONNA: | Nothing. |
| JIM: | Well, OK then. Look if you don't want to tell me fine, just don't get mad about it. |
| DONNA: | You know what, we are fighting. Do you want to know what you did? |
| JIM: | Umm, yes. |
| DONNA: | Do you? |
| JIM: | No. |
| DONNA: | I caught you trying to hide your wedding ring. |
| JIM: | What? |

| | |
|---|---|
| DONNA: | You were trying to hide your ring. You forgot that we were married and you had found your wedding ring on your hand so you thought you stole it. You didn't want to get into trouble so you were trying to hide it. |
| JIM: | I'm sorry. Have you already told me this? |
| DONNA: | This is the fifth time we've talked about this this morning. |
| JIM: | Where is my ring? |
| DONNA: | I'm keeping it, just to be safe. |
| JIM: | Sorry. |

## FEBRUARY

*DONNA is sitting on the couch, JIM comes past.*

| | |
|---|---|
| JIM: | Good night. |
| DONNA: | You're going to bed? It's six-thirty. |
| JIM: | Oh. |
| DONNA: | Are you tired? |
| JIM: | I guess no. |
| DONNA: | Sit down hun, relax. |

*JIM sits next to DONNA, he begins to rub her neck.*

God, that feels good. Do you feel that knot?

| | |
|---|---|
| JIM: | You work hard. |
| DONNA: | Hmm? |

JIM: I said you work hard.

DONNA: Thank you sweetie.

*They kiss.*

JIM: 'Kay I'm going to bed.

DONNA: What? You're not tired.

JIM: I don't know.

*DONNA goes over to JIM.*

DONNA: If you're just so set on getting into bed, maybe I should join you.

JIM: I don't know.

*JIM and DONNA start to kiss, it grows passionate.*

DONNA: That feels so good.

JIM: How long has it been?

DONNA: Long. I love you Jim.

JIM: I love you too…umm

DONNA: Oh god.

JIM: We should…go to bed…

DONNA: Oh Jim.

JIM: Oh…

DONNA: That feels good Jim.

JIM: I love you…umm…, uh, shuuh—

DONNA: Jim. Jim?

JIM: Umm.

DONNA: Say my name.

> *JIM is blank.*

Do you know my name? Oh god.

> *DONNA pulls away.*

JIM: You're…uhh…you're mine. You're beautiful.

DONNA: Jim…shut up. Kiss me. Just be quiet and kiss.

> *They go off to bed.*


AUGUST

> *DONNA is trying to get JIM to eat dinner. He is completely unresponsive.*

DONNA: You need to eat, 'kay? I don't care if you don't think you're hungry, all right, eat. Seriously, Jim, it's the one thing I expect you to do all day. Look, you like this, it's chicken. Fine.

I made a cake for today, will you eat that? It's chocolate, you like chocolate.

> *DONNA goes to get her birthday cake, the phone rings, she answers. JIM remains in the room, motionless, through the conversation.*

Hello? Oh hi. Thanks Cathie, it's sweet of you to call. Forty, can you believe it. Yeah, it's a big one. Thank-you. No, not really. I know it's…well with everything going on it just seemed easier to not make it a big deal, I'll have another birthday next year. Yeah exactly, he's all I need. Well…he actually made me dinner. Uh huh, and a cake. I know. Yeah we'd planned to go out but he surprised me with this whole thing tonight, dinner, flowers. It's perfect, and really seeing Jim happy for a night is the best kind of gift. Oh Cathie you know what, just a second, he just lit the birthday candles.

*To JIM.*

I'll be right there sweetie. No don't start singing yet, give me a sec.

*Back on the phone.*

Cath I should go. We should, that sounds great. *(To JIM.)* Jim, I thought we said no gifts.

*Back on the phone.*

I know, how spoiled. OK, I'll call you next week. Thanks, bye.

*DONNA hangs up the phone, she takes a moment.*

Jim, I have a present. I'm pregnant. I'm pregnant. Jim? I'm pregnant…Jim, I'm pregnant.

JIM: Really?

DONNA: Do you know what that means?

JIM: That I'm…I'm going to be a dad?

DONNA: Yes sweetie.

JIM: I'm, I'm I can't—

DONNA: We'll have a family. How do you feel?

JIM: I've never been happier! Donna? Come here.

*They embrace.*

Oh my God, you are the most, I just, as long as I can remember I wanted to be a Dad, I've always…

DONNA: How do you feel sweetie?

| | |
|---|---|
| JIM: | I am so, happy. Donna you're amazing! Oh, OK, I'm going to be good at this. All you need to do is just be happy and take care of yourself, and I'll take care of you and everything, I'll do everything. What is it? |
| DONNA: | What? |
| JIM: | Do we know what it'll be? |
| DONNA: | What do you think, what do you wish for? |
| JIM: | Well I mean you know anything, either, is perfect, but…a daughter. |
| DONNA: | It's a girl. |
| JIM: | Donna! What a perfect perfect perfect…thing. |
| DONNA: | Why a girl? |
| JIM: | Well I mean I never had sisters, and I wasn't really friends with girls in school, I didn't know you as a girl or my Mom as a girl, but, all of my favorite people in the world are women. And to get to raise one, a girl who's a bit like you and like me but all herself too, like both of us but better. That's just perfect, you know? |
| DONNA: | Yeah. |
| JIM: | To get to do that makes us better. |
| DONNA: | Are you happy? |
| JIM: | This is the best… |
| DONNA: | You look proud. |
| JIM: | Donna! We should celebrate. |
| DONNA: | Oh I have a cake. |

*DONNA goes to get the cake.*

| | |
|---|---|
| JIM: | I can't believe it. I used to worry that we wouldn't |

| | |
|---|---|
| | have this, that that, maybe I wasn't able to or I wasn't or…you can't,/ you can't… |
| DONNA: | /Want some cake Jim. |
| JIM: | Wait, Donna…you can't/ have, what happened, I thought you can't have kids. |
| DONNA: | /Tell me what else, what name should we pick? Your Mom's? |
| JIM: | Donna? I thought that you couldn't be, uh, get pregnant. You can't be. |
| DONNA: | I just— |
| JIM: | Donna. Are we having a baby? |
| DONNA: | No. |
| JIM: | But… |

*We see JIM recess.*

| | |
|---|---|
| DONNA: | I'm sorry. Jim I'm sorry. It was a joke. Jim don't go. Just, pretend. Let's pretend. I'm sorry I just, don't… It was a joke, Jim you smiled. You smiled! I'm sorry. |

# JANUARY

*JIM is sorting through a pile of mail. Picks up an envelope, yells to DONNA.*

| | |
|---|---|
| JIM: | Donna? Donna get in here. |

*DONNA rushes in.*

| | |
|---|---|
| DONNA: | Are you OK? |
| JIM: | Why's the hospital mailing my Dad? |

DONNA: Let me see that.

JIM: Dad's dead. Idiots.

DONNA: Jim.

JIM: If they want money, fuck 'em.

DONNA: You're in a pissy mood.

JIM: Well excuse me if I don't like getting my dead Dad's mail sent to me.

DONNA: Jim it's for you.

JIM: What?

*DONNA hands JIM the envelope back, pointing to the name.*

DONNA: That's your name.

JIM: Well no one fucking calls me James. That's my Dad's name.

DONNA: Let's see what it says.

JIM: Don't open my mail. Here, have the cable bill. Wait, why the hell are the bills all in your name?

DONNA: It's just easier. It all comes out of our accounts, it's the same account Jim.

JIM: I—

DONNA: Just open your letter.

JIM: James? You better call them and tell them I'm Jim.

*Reading the letter.*

"Dear Mr James blah blah blah…special request… extremely rare occurrences…" Hot shit Donna!

DONNA: What?

JIM: They want my brain.

DONNA: They what?

JIM: Yeah yeah, they say my brain's so unique and… they want to study me.

> *JIM puts the envelope down and begins to elaborate. DONNA reads the letter.*

You know my Nana always said I had a one in a million brain. Smart-ass doctors, they know a brain they want to study when they see one.

DONNA: Jim. I don't think—

JIM: Oh don't be jealous Donna. Not everyone has a brain worth studying.

DONNA: Jim, you should understand what they're asking for here.

JIM: My brain.

DONNA: Yes. When you die they want permission to dissect and study your brain.

JIM: Who do you think told them how smart I was? Probably Nana.

DONNA: We're going to say no to this.

JIM: No we're not. I want to do this.

DONNA: It's too weird, I'm not comfortable with this.

JIM: I want this.

DONNA: It's not just your decision, we have to talk about this.

JIM: It is my decision. This is, it's an honor.

DONNA: It's an honour for them to want to slice your brain

| | |
|---|---|
| | apart/ and talk about you like you're some bizarre case study, some freak? |
| JIM: | Yeah. What, freak? |
| DONNA: | No, I didn't mean freak. |
| JIM: | You're just jealous. You're just being a stupid bitch and you're jealous. |
| DONNA: | Jim. |
| JIM: | I'm going to the hospital, they can sign me up there. |

*JIM starts looking for his keys.*

Where are my keys? Where the fuck, Donna did you put my keys somewhere? Why do you keep hiding shit on me Donna? Stop hiding…you're just jealous. What? Fine I'll walk.

DONNA: Sweetie it's cold out.

*JIM storms out. DONNA collects herself. JIM returns with his jacket.*

JIM: If you would just give me back—

*JIM tries to put his jacket on, but in his upset state he can't navigate the jacket. He keeps trying to slide his arm through the arm-holes but can't figure it out. He is slowly spinning around, until ultimately he is just staring at the jacket, trying to figure it out.*

DONNA: Oh sweetie look. We made a mistake.

JIM: What?

DONNA: This is an old letter. It's for your Dad, see?

JIM: Oh yeah. But isn't that my…

DONNA: Yeah. Sometimes we get his mail.

JIM: OK.

> *JIM finally puts his jacket on, backwards.*

DONNA: Are you warm with your coat on?

JIM: I'll take it off.

> *JIM begins to leave.*

DONNA: Hang it up please.

JIM: I know.

> *As JIM leaves he crumples up the paper and leaves it on the table. DONNA throws it into the garbage.*

## OCTOBER

> *DONNA is clearing dinner plates, comes back in with ice cream.*

DONNA: Ice cream?

JIM: Thanks. Dinner was great.

DONNA: Sorry it was just chicken again, the day ended up getting away from me.

> *JIM eats his ice cream, grimaces and rubs his temples.*

JIM: Ahh, brain freeze.

DONNA: Slow down.

> *They eat their ice cream in silence.*

So, um, I talked to the doctor this afternoon and—

JIM: Are you OK?

DONNA: It was your neurologist actually.

JIM: Oh?

DONNA: He called with some news. About some of results from—

JIM: He called you?

DONNA: He wanted to talk to me so I could talk to you first. Jim…

JIM: Why would he call you? What is it?

DONNA: He says that he thinks it's—what's been happening with you is…it, it looks like Alzheimer's, Jim.

JIM: How does it look like Alzheimer's?

DONNA: He says that they can't diagnose it for sure, one hundred percent without, um, actually seeing your brain, but he says he's sure that's what it is.

JIM: This is… I'm thirty-eight.

DONNA: It's early. Early onset Alzheimer's.

JIM: Donna we're thirty.

DONNA: I know sweetie. I'm so sorry. He says it's rare but that it's starting to happen more and more. It happens. And, it runs in your family, you know your Nana had it—

JIM: When she was eighty! Do you remember what an ordeal she became? She lost her mind, everyday it was a new fucking trauma with her.

DONNA: But she was happy.

JIM: She just smiled, doesn't mean she was happy. How could she be happy, she didn't know who she was.

DONNA: I know.

JIM: But, how is it…so what, are there things, drugs for it?

DONNA: Yeah. He did say that usually when it's diagnosed in people young like you it develops pretty quickly, but that there are some things you can take to try to slow the effects.

JIM: Like what?

DONNA: Um something called…I can't remember, I wrote it down, we'll—

JIM: What the hell Donna? Why the fuck did he tell you? Why didn't he call me?

DONNA: I'm sorry Jim.

JIM: No, it's just/, it's bullshit—

DONNA: /He said that he thought it would be best for you to hear it when you're at home. In your own surroundings, that type of thing. We thought it'd be less jarring.

JIM: So this how it goes? I get to be treated like a child. When something happens you give me the dumb downed version with a bowl of fucking ice cream? He should've told me.

DONNA: I didn't mean to—

JIM: I'm thirty-eight years old.

DONNA: I know.

JIM: No, I'm sorry. It's not fair…for me to get mad at you.

DONNA: No, it's OK. Come here.

*They embrace.*

JIM: So?

DONNA: I'm so sorry we did it this way. The doctor wants us to come in tomorrow at two. He'll give us all

|        | the details and we'll, /you know, figure out what to do. |
|--------|---|
| JIM:   | /I have work tomorrow afternoon. Can I still work? Oh my god. |
| DONNA: | I don't know. Maybe we'll think of a way for you to work from home like me. |
| JIM:   | I can't work from home as a paramedic. |
| DONNA: | I don't know. |
| JIM:   | I know. |
| DONNA: | We've got plenty of time to figure it all out. I know it's a shock, but we'll figure everything out together. |
| JIM:   | Our ice cream's melting. |
| DONNA: | I'm sorry. |
| JIM:   | Thanks. |

*They eat ice cream. He grimaces.*

| DONNA: | Slow down. |
|--------|---|

*They eat ice cream in silence.*


# NOVEMBER

*JIM is alone, drinking, writing. DONNA enters.*

| JIM:   | Hey babe. |
|--------|---|
| DONNA: | Hi. |
| JIM:   | How was your thing? |
| DONNA: | Dinner was good. Rachel says hi. |

JIM: Hi.

DONNA: She sent along a get-well card.

JIM: *(Laughing.)* Oh, OK. Fuck. What a thought.

DONNA: She's being nice.

JIM: Guess I should try to get well.

*Writes something on his list.*

DONNA: What are you doing?

JIM: I'm listing things.

DONNA: What?

JIM: I'm listing. I'm making a list of things I'll be happy to forget.

DONNA: That's terrible.

JIM: I think it's great.

DONNA: Is this an exercises from that book?

JIM: No, this is completely all my idea.

DONNA: I don't think it's…what's made the list so far?

JIM: Well…Mom and Dad's accident of course.

DONNA: That's OK.

JIM: Us not being able to have kids, or us finding that out too late I guess. Some little dumb mistakes.

DONNA: I'm going up.

JIM: Did you know, when I was a kid I could be a real bully, like in elementary school.

DONNA: You what?

JIM: Who knows why, I was mostly nice but sometimes I

|         | would just be fucking mean. Just to some kids, like they didn't do anything, who knows? |
|---------|---|
| DONNA:  | Everyone kid has moments when they're mean. You can't sit here and punish yourself over the past Jim, that can't feel good. You're not a bully. |
| JIM:    | I want to forget about being a paramedic. |
| DONNA:  | Why would you want to forget that? |
| JIM:    | It's like, like I was practicing to be good at taking care of people, not just as my job but just generally. I used to expect that that would be what defines me. I expected something would happen, like us having a kid with a dissability, or, if you know Mom was bed-ridden, or if you had to have chemo or something. Stuff like that happens and it's random and yeah really terrible, but it would have been pretty OK because I was good at taking care of people. I never thought I'd be… So, be good to forget that. |
| DONNA:  | What else? |
| JIM:    | Lots of shit. You and Dan. Sorry. |
| DONNA:  | No, I'm sorry. You know, you remember that I'm sorry. |
| JIM:    | Yeah. I want to forget that whole year. *(JIM pours another glass of scotch.)* I'll getcha a drink. |
| DONNA:  | You're not supposed to drink. |
| JIM:    | I don't know. |
| DONNA:  | How much have you had? |
| JIM:    | I don't know. |
| DONNA:  | Let's not do this tonight. |
| JIM:    | Do what? |

DONNA: This list thing. Maybe we'll do it tomorrow.

JIM: No no no, I won't remember to do it tomorrow.

DONNA: Jim.

JIM: That's the plan anyway. *(JIM downs his drink.)* Drink Donna?

DONNA: Jim.

JIM: What else do I want to forget?

DONNA: Stop this and let's go to bed.

JIM: Not yet. Have a drink with me.

DONNA: I don't want one.

JIM: Fine, great, I'll drink yours for you.

DONNA: You're not supposed to be drinking, the doctor said alcohol is just going to aggravate this whole thing.

JIM: That's exactly the plan. We're drinking tonight and we'll, we'll aggravate this whole fucking thing. So when I wake up tomorrow and I can't remember what I did tonight or what we said, at least it'll be because of me. 'Cause I chose to drink and to not remember. 'Cause I did something I wanted to. Not just 'cause I can't…'cause it just fucking happened, 'cause who knows…but because I chose it.

*JIM takes a punishing drink.*

DONNA: Don't do this to yourself.

JIM: Why not? So I forget tonight? So…I feel like shit tomorrow? So what? I don't have to go to work. I got nothing to do but feel like shit all day.

DONNA: How about, I could stay up with you, and in the morning if you want to remember anything I can remind you.

| | |
|---|---|
| JIM: | Here then, you make a list too. |
| DONNA: | Jim I don't want to, I wouldn't know what to— |
| JIM: | I know it's different for you, but still, what would you pick? |

*DONNA doesn't write anything.*

It's not hard. It can be anything you want. Alright, I'll start your list for you.

*JIM writes something on the list.*

Why did they make Alzheimer's such a hard name to remember how to spell?

*DONNA smiles.*

There's the smile. Donna's world famous smile. Wouldn't want to forget that.

Hey, I'm going to forget how badly I'm fucking up your life Donna. It's selfish for me to want to forget that, but I really do. You got to know, drunk or not, I'm going to forget this.

| | |
|---|---|
| DONNA: | I know. |
| JIM: | So, just so you know, if you ever want to like, scream at me or something, or hit me, you can cause I'll just forget about it. Or if you want to lie to me about stuff it it makes it easier, you should. You could even leave me if you ever want. Sooner or later I'll just forget and you can get on with your life. |

*JIM goes to write something on his list.*

| | |
|---|---|
| DONNA: | Don't write that down. Look, I'm not going to forget you Jim, but all these poor things on your list, these things you don't like about yourself, I'm not going to remember any of that. I'll take with me just the best parts of you. All of the kind and sweet things |

|        | you've done, all of your achievements, everything that made you perfect for me. I get to keep those. |
|--------|---|
| JIM:   | Like, you're keeping me a secret? |
| DONNA: | No. I'll share them with everyone you know, I'll tell your life story, but just with the highlights. |
| JIM:   | You won't tell them about the list? |
| DONNA: | No, it will be like an, umm, you know how in someone's obituary the family tells the right version of someone's life? How in them everyone sounds perfect? That's how people will remember you because that's how I'll tell it. |
| JIM:   | Am I dying? |
| DONNA: | No, no. |
| JIM:   | 'Cause I'm already dead? |
| DONNA: | Sweetie no. |
| JIM:   | 'Cause I feel like death. |
| DONNA: | This isn't going to kill you Jim, this is something that you live with. You have decades and decades of life still to go. |
| JIM:   | Oh. Oh Fuck. I'm sorry. I'm drunk. I'm sorry. I'll go to bed. |

*JIM goes to leave.*

| DONNA: | Can I have your list. I'll hold on to it for you. |
|--------|---|

*JIM gives her the list.*

|        | Jim? |
|--------|---|
| JIM:   | Hmm? |
| DONNA: | I'm…take a Tylenol before you go up, drink a glass of water. |

JIM: Yeah.

*JIM leaves, DONNA reads his list.*

## EPILOGUE

*JIM and DONNA are finishing another game of crib.*

DONNA: Twenty-six.

JIM: Twenty-nine.

DONNA: Thirty-one for two, and the run is five.

JIM: You win. One more—

DONNA: No. I'm sorry but we need to go sweetie.

JIM: But—

DONNA: I know, but we have an appointment and we're running late, 'kay?

*JIM is blank.*

We can't just keep playing. Would you put your shoes on?

*DONNA speaks to the audience.*

Jim and I haven't recognized each other in months. Except there are times when we're playing crib and he'll say a joke I know he's been saying since he was a kid, or he twirls the spare peg in his fingers like he's done thousands of times, and I think I see my husband again. But Jim and I haven't just been playing a game: Jim is the game. And I lost because this isn't like crib. There's no path, no points, no end.

They expected us at the extended care unit at ten this morning. That was six hours ago. I wanted just one game, to remember him like that. But he kept wanting to play, and play, and play. He kept forgetting the dozens of games we'd already had, but, but the admissions nurse—Jim's new nurse—will only be there for another half hour. There just isn't any more time for this. This good-bye's been too long. And I need to do it today. It's taken me weeks to build up the nerve for this. Jim fell asleep on the couch last night and I just left him there. But if he doesn't go today, if he sleeps next to me in our bed and I feel him there, if I feel his body curl around mine and have his knees press into the back of my legs. If he lies high on the pillow like he does and his chins touches the top of my head those same shivers will run down my body and all of my resolve will slip away. I wish I was stronger, or better, but I'm not. They told me that after today I can't see him for a little while. They say it's so he can acclimatize to his new home, I'm scared that that is code for giving him time to forget me.

This must have been the most important year in Jim's life, and he'll forget it all. I don't know how I'll remember this year though. This may have been the most important year of my life, but maybe not. Because I can still go on to have a life. I could meet someone else. I'm not saying I want to, that's not why I'm doing this, but I know that I could. And I know that it's possible someone could meet me, and love me. But Jim? I'll always love him, but no one new ever really will. How could they? The nurses, and the other patients, they'll adore him. They'll think he's funny, 'cause he can still be very funny. And he's still very handsome, and sometimes he's so gentle. But that's so quick to come and go. That's not love. You can't love someone until you know them, and there's not much left of Jim to get to know. He's all but disappeared. He's just so unknowable. Unlovable.

*To JIM.*

OK. You look ready.

JIM: Just need my keys.

DONNA: It's OK, I'll drive.

JIM: How come?

DONNA: Well you don't know where we're going.

JIM: OK then.

*JIM gives her a peck on the cheek as he goes by.*

Thanks Donna.

*We see DONNA standing at the door.*

*The End.*

# Appendix A

Through the course of writing the play I interviewed members of an Early Onset Alzheimer's and Dementia support group. These verbatim sentences are theirs, and in the original production the text was incorporated into the sound design during scene transitions. I also imagine the actor playing Jim reading the sentences, in whatever order the director chooses, even randomly, during transitions.

*"When I was first diagnosed I thought, oh great, now it's all seeing talking animals and stuff for me."*

*"I found an old family video a few weeks ago, and when I watched it I realized it was the first time in years that I heard my husband speak in a full sentence without any stops or stutters."*

*"Sometimes I feel like a nurse, like I take her to the bathroom and stuff now. But also, we take baths together and I learnt how to shave her legs, and I feel more like a lover than I ever have."*

*"I feel bad saying it, but I'm embarrassed of him when we're out. I have to be super selective about who we can spend time around."*

*"I like surprises."*

*"I hate that, for some reason, he now hates to have children around. He used to love kids, but now he just swears at them under his breath. My guess is he's afraid of them."*

*"He used to hunt. The first thing I did was get rid of all of the guns around the house. He agreed it was a good idea. He was scared of what he may do too."*

*"It's tempting to allow yourself to insult him, but I tell myself I can't because an insult to him is like steam from a kettle. Maybe he can't grasp it but it still can really burn him."*

"When we left for the care unit he knew he would never come home. I've never seen someone so angry. He must have hated me so much."

"His world has become so incredibly small."

"They had no idea what was wrong with him, I was so stressed out about it I ended up going to a therapist for myself. It was my therapist who thought it may be Alzheimer's. She caught it, not his doctors."

"I shouldn't talk to you, I don't know what I'll say."

## Appendix B

*Jim Forgetting* premiered in Alberta. The former Premier Ralph Klein suffered with dementia, though this reference may not be accessible across provincial borders. You may wish to substitute with the following text:

DONNA: But you're right, I can read it out loud, to refresh your memory. OK?

JIM: OK.

DONNA: OK. "Case study number five. At an evening honoring Ronald Reagan, his wife Nancy found herself in the now all-too-common position of attempting to hide the aging ex-President's mounting, yet still secret, Alzheimer's disease. She had written his speech for him, crafting a semblance of his voice, organized in thoughts small enough for him to grasp"—

JIM: Can you start from the beginning? Please.